SIDE
GLANCES

SIDE GLANCES

N O T E S · O N · T H E
W R I T E R ' S · C R A F T

JOHN V. HICKS

THISTLEDOWN PRESS

SASKATCHEWAN WRITERS GUILD

Canadian Cataloguing in Publication Data

Hicks, John V., 1907-
  Side glances
  1st ed. --

ISBN 0-920633-38-2

1. Creation (Literary, artistic, etc.) 2. Creative writing. I. Saskatchewan Writers' Guild.
II. Title.

PN149.H43 1987   808'.001'9   C87-098103-X

Book design by A.M. Forrie
Drawing of John Hicks by Patrick Lane
Cover design by Robert Grey

Typesetting by Apex Graphics, Saskatoon

Printed and bound in Canada by
Hignell Printing Limited, Winnipeg

Thistledown Press Ltd.   Saskatchewan Writers Guild
668 East Place   Box 3986
Saskatoon, Saskatchewan   Regina, Saskatchewan
S7J 2Z5   S4P 3R9

This book has been published with the assistance of the Canada Council and the
Saskatchewan Arts Board.

9-26-90

To all of my fellows
old and young
who would write better if they (we) could
and who can't stop trying

'Tell me a story' is the oldest cry in the human heart.
TOM HARPUR

A poem begins with a lump in the throat.
ROBERT FROST

All the world's a stage.
SHAKESPEARE

Contents

Foreword

About five years ago I was in Toronto trying to write in a badly heated garret infested with cockroaches. Try as I would, I could not get going on my story. I had this great idea, but I thought maybe I'd save it for the next story. Or the next. On one particularly cold day while two of the landlady's friends down below were having a fight over a stolen bag of dope, I was huddled at the kitchen table in a state of advanced apathy. Should I (once again) attempt to drive my story out into the open, should I check for mail, or should I phone my friend Hart and moan about the desolate state of my imagination?

I went down and got my mail and there was the latest *FreeLance*. I opened the issue to the following words:

> Never save a good idea for a better time, a better market. Use it. Otherwise you may be conditioning yourself to believe the good ideas are few and should be hoarded. Spend your good ideas lavishly, and there will be more then when you need them. The factory grows in strength by producing. Another mystery of the subconscious.

The author of these words of advice, of course, is John Hicks. Try, if you will, to imagine their impact on me. It was as if there were someone around who understood my problem, had wrestled with it, and was willing to point the way. My guess is that a serious writer would consider the above snippet good advice no matter how advanced s/he was in this game we all play.

Side Glances is full of such advice. The book is written for beginning writers (of poetry *and* fiction) in search of guidance from an old pro. But I can't imagine any mature, well published pros who wouldn't be delighted with this book—if only to have their own side glances confirmed and carefully articulated.

Side glances, as I understand the term, are those thoughts writers have when they're not writing or thinking about a poem or story. They glance away from the object of contemplation long enough to think about writing itself. Some of Hicks' side glances are very brief and contentious:

> Characters are interesting only to the extent that they grate on each other.
>
> ❖
>
> The poet is somehow assumed to be talking about himself, the fiction writer about others.
>
> ❖
>
> The mere chopping up of lines does not change into poetry what is essentially prose.

In one of Hicks' longer pieces, a dialogue between two writers, Hicks challenges our beliefs about the usefulness of writers' groups, an old Saskatchewan tradition. In this piece, as in the snippets above, Hicks does not hesitate to voice unfashionable or heretical ideas. In fact, his attack on the writing group mentality is entitled "Anyone for Heresy?".

Most of his side glances, however, are what I would consult for moral support (getting unlocked, getting published, and not getting discouraged) or for learning how to trust imagination — my own and that of the reader. The ideal Hicks reader participates actively in discovering what the poet or storyteller has left out. Hicks encourages us as writers, then, to learn the art of suggestive — nay, seductive — presentation.

So many of us are accustomed to John Hicks' poetic voice: full of playful, elusive, musical and stately indirections. *I* know him as a plainspeaking lover of books and pizza. Readers of *Side Glances* will encounter this second persona, his other voice, the conversational one. His advice is as accessible as it is wise. We are lucky to have John Hicks' reflections on writing as near as our own bookshelf. They are almost as edifying (and delightful) as eating pizza with John Hicks.

David Carpenter
Saskatoon

Introduction

I have always been interested in writings about writing, and in the oral testimonies of established writers. I have kept these in mind, and I have jotted a lot of them down from time to time. Nothing within can be claimed to be highly original, except as it may reflect certain personal illuminations which have flared up as a result of their suggestions being passed on to me. I pass them on in turn. Nobody can learn to write by reading a book, but all can profit by being encouraged, and by being reminded that writing is a physical action brought about by a mental stimulus. For all our fine inspirations, our commendable intentions, we eventually have to sit down and do it. Thinking about it is much more comfortable, but doing it is what counts. Hemingway wrote standing up. Perhaps he was reminding himself that the thing finally translates into a job of work. Do it in any position you like, but get it done!

The contents of this book consist, in large measure, of short articles which have appeared in *FreeLance,* the journal of the Saskatchewan Writers Guild. My sincere thanks to Paul Wilson, whose idea it was that they be collected.

J.V.H.

THE CORNER OF MY MOUTH

Many books called (even by implication) *How To Write* might very well have been called *How I Write*. Exciting as these treatises may be, you eventually have to find out your own *how* for yourself; and the way to find it is by writing.

The artist (with words, brush, musical notation or whatever) is doing much more than entertaining an audience. He is working out a sort of turmoil in his creative mind — a turmoil of such compelling interest that it can be shared with an audience to the audience's advantage.

If you write in the third person, remember that you are not a mere reporter. It isn't much use telling the reader what your characters did and said. The characters should be there on the paper, showing themselves off. The reader is their audience. He doesn't need you.

Cultivate silence. Not concentration, just relaxed and total silence. Silence for its own sake. The stray words and phrases which intrude on this silence (and they will, in their own time) are your own creative material. Why else did they appear, why let you hear them in your secret heart? They are the gifts of the spirit.

Wall-to-wall carpet is death to sound, as all musicians know. The natural resonance of a lively room with hard floors is a physical pleasure to the ear drums, and no boosting up of volume will bring a dead room to life. Don't carpet your poems, either. They should reverberate in the mind's ear while they are being read. Language is sound.

Have you noticed that when a poem comes to you more or less in a piece, practically finished, it tends to contain few adjectives? This is because the meat and bones of it formed as a natural growth in your mind – and adjectives are not meat and bones. All too often they are sauce, garnish, filler. Meat and bones are nouns and verbs. That's what gives a poem real force and content. (Yes, I know, the first three dozen lines of *King Richard III* blossom with about as many adjectives. Is your name Shakespeare?)

There is a terrifying disease known, in one aspect and for want of a better term, as Writer's Block. The symptoms boil down to a complete creative freeze, an inability to put a single word on paper. Nothing will come. To treat this disease one should first understand what it is. It is really not a disease at all. It is a reason, served up by the subconscious, for not writing. It is an excuse in fancy dress. If writing is putting words on paper, then any literate person can write at the drop of a hat. A block is in no way a physical paralysis. You can still put words on paper. They don't have to be any good to qualify as writing, and right there is the secret of the treatment. If you are afraid you can't write a good story, you can certainly sit down and write a bad one – an utterly hopeless one that no editor would finish reading; the worst you can possibly do. The theory is that no one can write that badly indefinitely, and that if you keep it up you will, in due course, find some good and promising passage (i.e. idea) there in front of you. In the meantime you just keep pounding, or scribbling, too stubborn to quit. But you don't freeze.

Well established writers have often reported that if, on days when they simply don't feel like writing, they keep doggedly slamming it out anyway; then on looking this work over later they find the quality is not much different from that achieved on days when they were fired up. In other words, one great secret of the writing game is to keep writing.

SOFT WAX

That great story-teller Somerset Maugham once said that he couldn't be in a strange place for more than a couple of days without a story beginning to form around it in his mind. How is your sense of location? What mood would strike you at a small summer resort, closed for the season, with a chill October wind sighing around a deserted boat house? In a deep forest, coming suddenly upon the print of a long forgotten road? By the sea shore, a sound of dripping water echoing from the far recesses of a cave? And don't laugh at the old ruined house standing alone in the moonlight, the night breeze stirring up creakings in loose shutters. It still hasn't told half its stories.

❖

George Freitag, who painted signs and held creative writing sessions in California some years ago, once told one of his classes that to write a short story you need only put down a statement of fact, and move with it until the fiction begins to whirr of its own volition. Next time you are quite alone, sit down with that one for a few minutes. It might surprise you.

❖

Never save a good idea for a better time, a better market. Use it. Otherwise you may be conditioning yourself to believe the good ideas are few and should be hoarded. Spend your good ideas lavishly, and there will be more then when you need them. The factory grows in strength by producing. Another mystery of the subconscious.

❖

When you are inspired with the beginnings of a story, it is your own deep secret. Keep it. You talk about it at your peril. The need to communicate it may be satisfied if you tell it out loud. Tell it privately to your typewriter, and keep it private until a first draft is finished. Maintain the tension, the driving force, intact.

❖

The way to get ideas is to be the kind of person to whom ideas come. It isn't a conscious search, necessarily. You need inside you a soft-wax area that will take an impression the moment something touches down on it. You put your brains to work after that, not before.

❖

Taking a poem apart to find out what it is made of is a dangerous experiment. You may very well come to the conclusion that it isn't made of anything. What is a peal of bells made of? (Not the bells, but the peal.) A poem is to a great extent an effect. By and large, by the way, so is a story.

❖

Haiku purists insist that when you write haiku you must not say anything poetic. The whole idea in that tricky little three-line poem is to bring to the reader's attention a couple of observed ingredients which will awaken his mind to a poetic experience. It is the reader who becomes poetic.

❖

Writing generates writing. You'll find that some of your most inventive touches may appear while you are in the act of writing. You'll look back on them and wonder how such ideas ever came to you. Sitting thinking is all very well, but sitting writing can be productive. Write!

WHATEVER HAPPENED TO THE SOAP BOX?

A story is an emotion that has found a metaphor.

❖

Characters are interesting only to the extent that they grate on each other.

❖

The poet is somehow assumed to be talking about himself, the fiction writer about others.

❖

The mere chopping up of lines does not change into poetry what is essentially prose.

❖

A poet needs readers, to tell him what he was saying.

❖

Your past, in every significant detail, is sitting waiting patiently to get through to you.

❖

Gaze at a clear prairie sky. Don't concentrate on it. Let *it* concentrate on *you*.

❖

A well rounded poem is like a sphere. It is impossible to view it completely.

❖

A meteor is nothing but a bit of burning garbage from space. Oh? Don't you believe it. Your imagination can do better than that.

❖

Never rush a new piece of work into the mail. It will be better tomorrow than it is today; better still with a day in between.

SOME ASPECTS OF DAWN

It is said by some to be the most beautiful word in the language. Its structure is interesting. It begins with an attack and ends in infinity, and its vowel is subdued and somewhat shaded. Singers have confidence in such a word because they know exactly where it begins, and they can either cut it off with a pleasurable snip or let it nasal away into the distance as occasion may demand. When you begin with words like *love, move, never,* etc., say singers, you have to begin them a moment before the beat and set the beat itself down on the vowel, thus giving the word in question its proper emphasis and shape. With *dawn,* though, the tongue knows its exact point of attack; and the vowel, neither the brightest nor the blowiest, sits comfortably on the face.

This sense of attack is strange, because dawn as we know it is by nature so indefinite. Whoever first thought of the expression 'the break of day' was obviously all wrong. The last thing in the world day does is break. At what precise moment does dawn announce itself? No one knows, unless perhaps the meteorologists have some sort of official fracture which can be noted on their charts, one day to another. Dawn happens. We know it is there, but not when it came.

Stories, poems, plays are like that in their beginnings. The best way to come up with an idea is to let it happen. It is inadvisable, usually, to frown and determine to hammer out a story about a boy and a girl and a barbecue, and a commercially manufactured tomahawk lying on the ground beside them. It is better to relax and ponder why they popped into your mind at all; to let their quiet presence begin to draw on every reaction you ever had to everything that ever happened, to everything that ever took place in your unrecorded experience. You wait for the slightest clue. You note the special kind of smile and toss of the head as a single curl of briquette smoke takes the girl by the right nostril, and how the boy shapes his silent and barest snicker, and how their relationship is already circling the fire on tiptoe. They will speak when they are ready, and you will listen to the first soft words they say.

The tomahawk? You didn't know it, but the tomahawk lying on the ground is a symbol of something. It points somewhere. Not in any narrative direction, necessarily, but inward to some truth of which you didn't know you were aware. Without it, or with some other object, it might well be another story. *Be still, still.* You aren't ready to make a comment yet. Whatever the idea may be, you are letting it dawn. It is a shapeless thing, and may very well remain so for a lengthy interval. It will reveal itself all in good time if you don't go looking for it. If you let it come looking for you. You are involved there somewhere yourself, never mind why. You are going to show the shape and significance of the person you are, after you can contain it no longer and have given up and decided you must spill the beans to a reader.

The mystery is that elements tend to attract each other and come together in the mind, or jell, without your knowing. But you will know when they do. You will hear, almost, the tell-tale click. The idea will have dawned, and when it has it will produce that faintly percussive *d*.

Or, try it this way. Some little certainty, or fixation, that has been roosting in your mind for a long time, suddenly contacts some commonplace thing that will serve to illustrate it, and the light grows without your noticing.

Moods are fertile ground for the germination of ideas. What emotions, recollections, might steal over you in the following settings?

A deserted farm house, falling into decay.

Waking on a sports day to the sound of rain.

Waking and remembering it is Saturday. Monday.

A tearful argument in the next room, midnight.

A boy and a girl and an old man, sitting in a cafe.

A crippled woman toiling patiently along a street, smiling.

The shapes of words are yours, too, and how they fall, and in what order and rhythm. An experienced reader can tell Lois Simmie from Ken Mitchell, from Rudy Wiebe, from Gertrude Story, even if they all use an identical list of words. After a few hundred thousand words are

17

behind you, no one will write quite like you.

To get an idea, let's repeat, you must be the kind of person to whom ideas come. You don't go poking about in the underbrush with a stick. You keep strolling through the woods, and all sorts of living things, things dimly remembered or believed forgotten, may get quietly to their feet and overtake you.

There is no such thing as the crack of dawn.

ANYONE FOR HERESY?

Les Crackham turned on me a quizzical eye, at an angle that suggested he was in one of his controversial moods. Les will take any side on any subject, when he's so minded, just for the pleasure of trying to jockey you into a corner. He fondled a black briar pipe as he spoke.

"Why," he asked "are you writers so keen on getting together and criticizing each other's manuscripts?"

"I'll bite," I replied. "Why do I brush my teeth?"

"All right, why do you?"

I shrugged. "It's the thing to do."

"Precisely. The toothpaste boys spread the word long ago that you must get all those food particles out from between you teeth, whereas what really matters is diet and good bone."

"Enamel," I said.

"Okay, however you like it. But you and a billion others go right along without question."

"Aren't you forgetting you mentioned manuscripts?" I asked.

"No, I'm not. You people sit around passing judgement on each other's work because someone told you it's the thing to do. Well, for the beginner who can't put an effective sentence together, maybe it is. But for writers who really write, it's all bird-chirp."

"You're shoving your wrecking bar under a great tradition," I said. "If criticism's so bad, what else would you suggest?"

"I didn't say criticism was bad," he insisted. "I'm merely suggesting that criticism by other writers isn't worth a hoot."

"Why not? Don't they know from experience what will work and what won't? Aren't they the most likely people to sense when a story is taking a wrong turn?"

"Nuts," he said. "They don't know anything from experience. Every yarn is a brand new start. The fact that they did it once doesn't mean they can keep on doing it over and over at the drop of a hat. The fortieth story is as hard to write as the second."

19

"You sound like a writer," I said.

"Well, it's true. How can there be a *way* to write a story? And if there is, there can't be anything but your own personal way, based on who knows what. Attitudes, reactions, opinions, the whole bit—everything you have lived with up to now. Another writer will see the whole thing quite differently."

"And isn't all that variation worth while? All that fellowship—"

"Fellowship," he said, "is the best reason in the world for getting together. Perhaps it's the only reason—the only good one, anyway. It makes for inspiration. It says look, we're all doing it and somehow we can keep on doing it. Great."

"And you think a bit of friendly criticism spoils it all?"

"I simply think the criticism of other writers is useless, which is what I was saying just now. The moment you show a script to a group of writers, each one in turn begins to want to correct it. He sees only the way he'd have written it himself, if he'd been the author. His whole life background rears up and begins to rewrite the thing in his mind. He only knows *his* way. He can't look at a script objectively."

"So what do we do at our next writers' meeting—sit around and chew the ribbon?"

"Exactly. Talk about everything under the sun. Enjoy each other's company. Then go home and make a run for the typewriter. You're back where you belong, working more wordage out of your system, refining your writing as only more writing will. You'll find out all in good time that what you wrote last week was no masterpiece. It may take another ten thousand words, or fifty, but you'll find out."

"So we end all round-the-circle criticism, huh?"

"Not quite. But if you must have criticism, use a group whose opinions will make sense."

"Like?"

"A group of voracious readers, naturally. People who have been reading fiction for years just because they enjoy reading fiction. They are your right and proper critics. Show them your yarns, and you instantly have thousands of hours of experience working for you, right from your potential audience. And ask them three questions."

I raised my eyebrows, knowing he'd go on anyway.

"Write your three questions on a slip of paper, and let each reader answer with an anonymous tick: 1. Did you thoroughly enjoy this story? 2. Did you find it only partially interesting? 3. Did you feel like giving up, and if so by what page?"

There was a tiny squeak as he removed the lid from a heavy glass humidor and began a ceremonial packing of the bowl of the black briar he was holding. I sensed the discussion was drawing to a close.

"I'll bring up your idea before the next writers' meeting," I said. "It should cough up quite a little storm."

"Don't overdo it," he advised, grinning. "Some of my best friends are writers." He shot me a puckish glance. "And some of them earn money doing criticisms."

That was another angle, but I didn't try to explore it. He gave the rich bowlful of tobacco a loving tamp or two, struck a match, and began carefully applying the flame.

THE SMELL OF YESTERDAY

According to a recent newspaper filler, of the five human senses the sense of smell is most closely linked to memory. Newspaper fillers have a reputation as self-starters for writers; that one should send you scampering for your clip-board, whipping out your pencil or ball-point as you go.

Make a list of the smells that are uppermost in you memory, distant, recent, or both. They may run all the way from skunk to Chanel No. Five. For what particular scene or set of circumstances do you remember them? That sea shore at low tide? Peeling oranges around the kitchen table? Cutting up meat for the freezer? Gutting trout? Charred timbers in that burned shack? An old attic? A root house?

Who was with you at the time? What happened? What *might* have happened? Any suggestion of conflicts, stresses, emotions? The moment you begin entertaining emotions and stresses, you are fooling around with the stuff of fiction. In this case you are plowing your inner self for material.

Let's put down a bit of off-the-cuff schmaltz as a story opening suggested by the sense of smell:

> June, and the first scent of wild roses on the air. Grover thought he should board a plane midway through that painful month and not come back until the frail blossoms had had their day.

No, don't rush to the typewriter. Let the atmosphere simmer. What other character might fit on the stage, opposite Grover? What was on his mind? Might anything still happen to continue an action?

Let's try again:

> Thompson paused, frowning. There was that same smell, the one he had never been able to trace to its source. Not quite perfume, not quite decay. He had sworn it must be coming from

22

the cupboard under the stairs, but every time he opened the door the smell disappeared.

What do we have here, a flesh-crawler?

Perhaps you don't believe that newspaper filler. Perhaps you think some other sense, say the sense of sight, is stronger in the memory. Let's go along with that:

> The big Percheron came barrelling out of the barn and took off at a dead gallop. "Whoa, boy!" Hart yelled, but the horse was in full flight, wild-eyed, taking the gate at a leap and disappearing over the rise of ground. Hart stood poised, glancing at the kitchen door of his shack and wondering whether he'd make it if he had to run for his life.

If your clip-board has half a dozen sheets in its grip, as any writer's clip-board should, you ought by now to be luring any number of memories into the area of the imagination. There are still three senses left. Sense of touch, for instance. One of Walter de la Mare's poems, a delicate Christmas-and-mistletoe bit, ends like this:

> stooped in the still and shadowy air
> lips unseen, and kissed me there.

A romance novel waiting for an author?

The sense of hearing could save your life. You are suddenly alert at three a.m., wondering what wakened you. Then it comes again—the faintest tapping sound. You are alone with the breath of menace on your ear drums.

Well, what do you make of that? How serious might it be? Was the expectation of it lurking somewhere amongst your fears? Don't shrug it off. Play around with it for a couple of hundred words, or three.

What is your sharpest memory related to the sense of taste? A picnic? Opening the emergency rations? Breakfast in jail? There you have three senses about as varied as you could get. How were you involved in each? If you weren't involved at all, how *might* you have been? Or, do you know someone who was?

We have strayed somewhat from our newspaper filler concerning the sense of smell. Never mind. Snout to the trail, we may by now be sniffing at the elusive scent of a story. Or, for that matter, a poem.

THE THIRD AUNT MARY

It was raining, and I was six. The kitchen window admitted a wan grey light. Outside, the misery of a sodden landscape. Saturday morning and nothing to do. I was under my mother's feet.

She said, "Why don't you write a letter to Aunt Mary?"

Resistance began tightening around my vitals. The prospect was even worse than a wet day. I dug in and balked. Then I asked the question that has threatened to abort many a writing career. Screwing my face into the contour of a pretzel, I blurted: "What'll I say?"

Lesson One. You never ask, "What'll I say?" You say it. You put it down on paper and look at it. If it isn't worth saying, what's a waste basket for, anyway? Say something else, and else, and else, and eventually something will have to happen. In this business of making a start you don't need help; you need stubborn persistence.

But back to Aunt Mary. Suppose I had decided to give it a whirl, and had picked up a piece of paper and a pencil and begun:

> Dear Aunt Mary. It is raining, and I can't find anything to do, so I thought I would write you a letter.

Now then, what sort of Aunt Mary, reading that, do you think would sniff sharply, toss the letter down, adjust her cuffs, and say to herself, "Hah. Can't think of anything else to do, so he writes me this letter."

What sort of Aunt Mary do you think would lower the letter, look toward the ceiling, crinkle her eyes, give her face over to a sunburst smile, and chuckle, "Well, isn't that just priceless?"

Now notice a remarkable thing. From those two brief snatches, you have in your mind's eye a complete picture of Aunt Mary, haven't you? You could almost describe each of them on the spot, couldn't you? Angular or plumpish, tall or medium, voice, shape of hands, colour of hair and how she wears it, how she'd get in and out of a chair, of a car,

24

of a coat. You'd recognize each if you met her on the street. What if you met her in a cafe, in a pub, at church, breakfast, a ball game?

Dear me, these people are real to you already and you haven't made a move. 'Creating a character' is more or less a technical term. In actual writing practice, characters tend to present themselves, often in one quite irrelevant flash, and you have to have the eye, ear, wit, to realize them quickly before they slip away.

Next step. Write down another possible response to the opening of that kid's letter. Think up one of your own, quickly, off the cuff. What sort of Aunt Mary would react like that? Well, go ahead—describe her. You must have seen her and formed a sharp impression of her. Put it all down. Ask yourself how she goes about her household tasks or her trade or her profession; what sort of temperament she displays at a meeting of her women's association, at a party, a bridge game, a careless accident, anything you like.

Note that there is something special about this third Aunt Mary. She is *yours*. She appeared to no one else.

But, you say, I don't want to write children's stories.

Who said anything about children's stories? All you've been doing is letting two or three characters happen. You are at this moment standing at the very dead centre of creative writing itself.

Ask a hundred writers where they get their ideas, what this thing is all about, what material they use, and ninety-nine of them will mention people, characters, in some way. If the other one said he was a writer he was lying.

Stories are people. People react upon each other. They create tensions between each other, hates, loves, deceits, jollifications, murders, as a result of their particular personalities. Personalities make stories.

One more thing, a warning. Fictional people will resist with all their might doing what you tell them to do. They prefer to do their own thing, the thing that comes natural to them. If you expect to write about them successfully you had better watch closely, and listen attentively, and record it all faithfully.

Your Aunt Mary has to be real, after all.

SIDE GLANCES

Did you at any time, last winter, sit at a window and look out on a frozen lake? A frozen field, perhaps? If you did, what sensation took you? Did you feel perished, wishing for summer, longing for spring? You missed the boat. You ought to have felt the stillness of the mind. When the mind is still, activity suspended, creative thoughts are free to present themselves, unimpeded by hurry, tension, emotional turmoil. If you live to see next winter, look out of a window overlooking a frozen lake. A frozen back yard, even, might do.

There are two senses to the word *compose*. We may say to a het-up friend, "Compose yourself." To compose is to invite relaxation. On the other hand, to compose is to create. Perhaps as writers we have to learn to reconcile the two. We have to learn that creativity will begin to flow if we don't tense up and constrict it. Biting your nails is fear — fear that you won't succeed. Compose yourself while you compose.

How soon after the opening of your story will your reader be able to answer the question, "What's up?" How soon will he or she settle down to enjoy what you yourself are up to? What is there on page one that will urge a reader on to page two? Make it an effort to turn the page, and you've just lost a reader. Curiosity, expectation, satisfaction — go to work on the reader with words like these. The Reader, always the Reader...

In any piece of writing the author is the third dimension. A script may lie flat on the page, so long and so wide, but in the hands of an imaginative writer it will rear up and become a kind of edifice. It will have cubical contents as well as area dimensions. It becomes something you can get inside. You find yourself living in it. In other words, the author is not telling you, but rather showing you. A continuing sense of discovery is what keeps a reader reading.

❖

Time spent developing sheer technical skill is time well spent. You may have the liveliest ideas, but can you write a nicely put sentence, a well constructed paragraph, a verse that compels the ear? Henry Rago, once editor of *Poetry Magazine*, said that good writing should stand up off the page and have *vibration*. Look for this vibration in all the first class writing you read, whether verse or prose. It is the way the words seem to quiver for a moment in the pit of your stomach.

❖

The following may be a wacky bit of mathematics, but it would be difficult to argue down. If a publication receives a thousand manuscripts a month for consideration, including yours, it is a mistake to decide gloomily that your chances of acceptance are one in a thousand. The fact is that when an editor reads your script he either wants it or he doesn't. It is yes or no. Therefore your chances are always fifty-fifty. Wacky or not, this little calculation carries its own message. Give an editor something so good, so right for his pages, that he won't want to reject it, and you are somewhere on top of the heap.

SEEING IS BELIEVING

A well known novelist of some years ago said that you should write your story as though it were being acted out in front of you on a brightly lit stage. In other words, telling the reader what happened is in no way as effective as bringing him into the action and letting him see and hear for himself. Don't shove your characters off stage and attempt to report it all second hand. The reader may never quite believe you, but he will believe your characters if you get out of the way and let them perform. Which of the following sparks more interest?

> 1. He hurried over and told Joe Button in no uncertain terms to get lost.
> 2. His knuckles rapped a tattoo on Joe Button's door. When it opened he said, "Look, fella, I've had all your butting in I can take. Get lost, will you?"

No. 1 is mere reporting. No. 2 makes you an eye witness to a confrontation, with hostility about to explode. You can see Joe swinging the door wide and stepping forward with his teeth showing, can't you?

It is also a good idea periodically to show your characters in some simple action during a conversation. It keeps them on stage where the reader can see them. Like this:

> The *scritch* of the match as he lit a cigarette held me in suspense as to what his answer would be.

"Positioning" your characters at the outset of a story, showing them in a close-up setting, is another way of bringing them alive at once:

> His headlights picked out the body of the girl spread-eagled across the yellow line.

When you write a poem you should try never to name sensations, never to declare openly how you yourself feel. You must try to stir in the reader the emotions you are experiencing. Yeats said:

> Nine bean-rows will I have there, a hive for the honey bee,
> And live alone in the bee-loud glade.

Can you make a comment or two on the solitude, the utter silence, expressed in those lines? Is there another instance in which the word "loud" has been used to express silence so effectively?

Incidentally, Yeats, in a letter to a friend, complained with some bitterness that none of his critics apparently noticed what great care and attention he gave to technique in his poems. Perhaps this was an unwitting compliment—the technique didn't show. To what extent is technique a mechanical thing? Weigh your answer carefully.

Poets know that the overuse of adjectives tends to weaken one's writing. Fiction writers know the same thing of adverbs. Take, for instance, three common enough adverbs: *gloomily, gaily, pompously*. Tack "he said" or "she said" on to the front of each, and you are in fact being perfectly clear. The trouble is, you are short-circuiting your writing. You are telling the reader what to think. How much better to put the reader on the scene and let him discover the feeling for himself, like this:

> *Gloomily.* He slouched to the window and stood looking out, head lowered, shoulders hunched, silent.
>
> *Gaily.* She wrinkled her nose at him, touched a finger to his cheek, and did a little dance towards the window.
>
> *Pompously.* He rose, adjusted his waistcoat, set his features into place, and began to speak.

You should take little snapshots of your characters and their actions at every opportunity. Seeing is believing.

'Summer is icumen in/ Loud sing cuckoo.' One wonders what causes these anonymous ballads and songs to survive, riding the centuries long after they have shed the names of their authors. Can what you write, in the long run, be more important than who you are? Would you wish to create a line, or a character, so vivid as to be remembered by the reading public after you yourself are forgotten? It's a sobering thought. Anyway, take it with you to your summer school of the arts, or your lakeside cottage, or your backyard umbrella, and good scribbling!

TOUGH IT OUT

In a race between imagination and language, imagination will win every time. It flies unhindered by rules and restrictions. It is a pointless victory, however, because there is no prize and no audience to cheer. It has to wait for the slower footsteps of language to catch up. What this silly parallel is trying to suggest is that the act of language catching up to the imagination is what is meant by craft. A writer may be able to shake good ideas out of his sleeve, but they won't get anywhere unless he knows how to shape them up, give them point, put them on paper so that the reader will be drawn in, involved, and finally convinced.

Study your craft. How? Read a story by an author you admire. Then tell yourself the story line so it is firmly fixed in your mind. Now read the story again, this time noting every detail that held your interest as you read it. What made you want to keep on reading after the first few opening lines? What incidents were presented in a gripping manner as compared to a mere statement of them? What made you see in your mind's eye the various bits of action? What single words were lively instead of casual, exactly fitted to what they were describing or conveying? How does all this affect your feelings, your emotions? Do you care what happens or is going to happen? Does the ending convince you that this is what had to happen?

Now, if you have the patience, you might like to go for a work session. Sit down and write the story yourself, being careful not to copy bits of the original. Start, if you like, from some different angle or from some other point in the narrative. Don't stop until your own version is finished.

See how much you have to learn? To conduct ten such experiments, say, would be to give yourself a season's exercise from which only good could come. (Bear in mind, of course, that these experimental stories are not yours. Don't try to attach your name to them.)

31

Writing is hard. This, as one author of half a century ago observed, is in fact an encouraging thing. If it were easy everybody would be doing it, and getting into print would be no more than a sort of sweepstakes. You have to tough it out. Incidentally, no matter how famous you may live to become, the evidence is that it will always be hard. Margaret Laurence once said that her greatest fear was the blank sheet of paper, the fear that she might never be able to fill it. (She usually did.)

I possess a thick silver medal from the Crimean War. It belonged originally to a friend of my grandfather. I can take it out of its plush-lined case, and handle it, and recall the details of the exciting old seafaring yarn connected with it. And so I understand perfectly what Archibald MacLeish meant when he said a poem should be

> Dumb,
> As old medallions to the thumb.

Have you a curio or two, tucked away somewhere, over which you can rub your thumb? Ideas lurk everywhere. A sensitive thumb may very well have the power to call one up. By the way, what do you suppose is the significance of that word *dumb*?

John Ciardi once said that free verse is only easy to write badly. That one should sit us all down for a few moments' reflection. As we veer away from strict scan and rhyme, the need for a fine control increases if anything.

WELL UP

The made-to-order plots have all run out. Years ago certain suppliers of story plot outlines used to set them up for you like prescriptions on a pharmacist's counter, and you put the ingredients together and *presto*. They gave you long lists of suggested characters (teacher, farmer, philosopher, etc.) and one-word descriptions (kind, malevolent, saucy, etc.) and dramatic situations (to overcome hatred, to prevent a loss, etc.) and other categories like setting, complication, climax and what-not. You were left on your own then to fill these things in, or out, one by one. It took a long time for the amateur fraternity to realize that the stories thus produced all had a similar ring and a shallow depth-measure.

The trouble is that a story may not be made up of definite ingredients. More often than not, the narrative represents the growth (or deterioration) of an interesting character. Ingredients may be the things that surface after the mind is through composing. You read the finished work and you find out what it was made of. The mind was busy creating it (click-click and carriage bell) without consulting the writer as to the ingredients.

Indeed, very often a story simply wells up, a product of the writer's personal attitude towards a scrap of information or a bare idea, and it may very well prove to be a much better story than one which is deliberately put together out of so much this and so much that. You can adjust its actual ingredients afterwards if necessary (for creation often needs fixing after the fact) but it is difficult to lay out a pile of materials and then begin to create. In construction work, for instance, it is the architectural idea that dictates the materials and not the other way round.

You must learn to trust the sometimes apparently bungling creative mind. It will in due course make itself clear and tell you what it wants.

Can we make stories well up? Chekhov suggested that we can persuade them to. He said if you stare at any object long enough, even though it be a blank wall, a story will appear out of it—even out of the wall.

This is crystal ball stuff, and there's no denying it fits in with the curious nature of the subconscious mind—which is our native territory, after all. Concentration on *nothing* might be the key. Stare at anything you like, relax until your mind is blank, blank, blank, and wait for the very first thought that drifts in. Who knows, it might be a gift from the universe. One thing is certain. A story that came to you out of a wall would be *your* story, wouldn't it?

❖

It is understandably difficult for editors to say just what it is they are looking for, although they will recognize it right away when they see it. What they don't want is much easier to express. Poetry editors have from time to time noted down some of their pet hates. They don't want to see things like this in submitted manuscripts:

> Editorializing. Don't sound off.
> Contrived phrases. Be sincere.
> Ineptness, which one editor declared to be the only taboo.
> Rhyme for its own sake. Rhyme, when used, should be natural.
> Lines that sound like arranged prose.
> Everyday sentiments rehashed.
> Faulty grammar, bad spelling. Learn to use your tools.
> Merely descriptive pieces. Tie it to something.
> Lack of vitality and fresh images.
> Personal feelings. It is the reader who should feel.

❖

Want more mileage out of your carbon paper? Slice about a quarter of an inch off a sheet of carbon when it begins to dim. If you type double-space, as of course you should, and if you begin each page a standard distance down from the top, this will position your typing line in between the former carbon lines, and you'll be typing on fresh carbon paper.

CRY ON MY SHOULDER

You can't just find out how to write and then live happily ever after, even though practitioners of the art declare it to be the happiest life one can enjoy. Any happy-ever-after connected with writing comes from the achieving of conquest after conquest, the periodic wresting of victory from reversal after reversal. Even victory is usually tempered by the knowledge that you might have done better. The final product may never quite measure up to the first fine vision you had of it, and you'll look at it and decide it will simply have to do. If you did your best, maybe your best will be better next time. This is not wishful thinking. It is the creative drive getting primed for another push.

The intervals between victories can be distressing. Alice Munro, believe it or not, said: "Sometimes the right words can't seem to get on paper. My mind is either cluttered or empty. A story is all trial and error, every time I sit down to write one. I don't think you train to be a writer. It's out of your powers."

There you have a noted author suffering a bit of despair. Lesson? When despair overtakes you, tell yourself that you can, and will, write your way through it. Don't let the typewriter or pen stop talking. The imp that is for the time being chilled to the bone will eventually warm up and deliver something.

Janice Elliot: "A novelist can no more tell you how to write than a wizard can tell you how to fly. The only way to write is to write."

Composer Igor Stravinsky, who exercised such a powerful influence on the whole of twentieth century music, declared that he worked whether he felt like it or not. Inspiration, he said, is a force brought into action by effort, active effort. (Read that sentence again.)

How many famous authors have said much the same thing? When Somerset Maugham was asked what he did when he couldn't think of anything to write, he said that he sat and wrote *W. Somerset Maugham* over and over until something better turned up.

Howard Engel: "The process of writing leads to ideas that wouldn't occur were you to just sit and think. You get ideas that seem to come out of the typewriter at you."

Most writers have from time to time looked back over a piece of writing and wondered how they ever thought of this idea or that expression. The truth is that the mind was busy inventing *while they were writing.* Some one of them said that before you can produce anything you must first have some words to look at. Sound ridiculous? Well, try putting twenty words on paper, or fifty, and then sit back and ask yourself what they mean, where they might go. Write down a single word that you find attractive, and see if you can throw some ideas around it.

If you need one thing in the blue-eyed world beyond a certain native talent, it is quiet determination. Hope springs eternal in no human breast more than in a writer's.

Can you find out how to write? Francois Mauriac said, "Every novelist ought to invent his own technique. That is the fact of the matter."

Norman Levine said of writing that it is essentially yourself. You have to go inside and find yourself, find your own material, find your own method of working.

❖

A market note from Greenwillow Books, New York, contains a sound bit of general advice. Aimed primarily at writers for small children, their suggestions might well apply to any aspiring author in any field:

> Read widely in your chosen area.
> Try to figure out why you like the works you like.
> Find the individual voice behind each work you admire.
> Find your own voice, and write.

IT'S MY IDEA

Probably many poets have felt the dreadful sensation that steals over the whole body, leaving it momentarily limp, when someone says why don't you write a poem about this, or about that, or here's something you could make a poem of. Just referring to it, right now, puts a knot in the stomach. There are two things wrong here. First, the proffered gift is usually something we wouldn't dream of writing a poem about, not for one blessed minute, and we despise it as we despise the insinuation that we are a machine waiting to process anybody's proposals. Second, we might very well have begun a poem about that very thing *if we had thought of it ourselves*. Had we thought of it for ourselves, it would have seemed original, at least for long enough to allow us to absorb it and apply our own private angles to it. The writing of poetry (or anything else) is nothing if not personal and private. In its earliest manifestation it has to spring from the writer and no one else.

Now, perhaps this bit of crab-meat is not to the liking of all. Perhaps the poet figure is overdoing it, telling us that ideas are not like birds looking for some place to perch, but rather eggs hatching. Whose side are you on? Take it to your next writers' meeting. It might stir something up.

❖

One thing you should do if you want to assess people is watch their motions, their gestures. These have become largely involuntary and may therefore be considered to express character in subtle and silent ways. In this light, pay particular attention to the movements of your story's characters. Use them to flash messages on the reader's mental screen. What could you express by that distinctive walk, that quick bird-like shift of the head, that constant changing of position in a chair, that freely waving arm, fingers stroking the chin, drumming on a table top, pulling at an ear lobe, clenched white-knuckled?

❖

It has been well said that after you have envisioned a story character you should not begin to commit him to actions too soon. The theory is that once you employ him in some definite activity you will stop probing into his character. This makes a lot of sense, because it is out of the fully realized character that innumerable story possibilities will spring. What is this character of yours really like? What is his background? What might he do under certain influences? Why? How might he react in certain situations? Why? How well can you get to know him as a person before you ever think of a story? Take your time. Intimate friendships are never formed instantly. Your story will grow as your attachment to its characters grows.

Someone once suggested that the reading and writing of poetry in adolescence is a kind of balm for loneliness. Certainly the deep-seated loneliness of the adolescent is no secret, as witness some of the poems submitted in school literary contests. Perhaps one who wants to go on to become a poet should remember to carry a bit of it with him, always. Perhaps no writer in any medium should ever seek to cleanse himself entirely of the loneliness of his youth. Nobody can help you create. Creation rises out of your own built-in sense of loneliness.

Terry Heath once observed, at a writers' gathering, that all creation comes out of chaos. Writers, read again the first three verses of the book Genesis, and note what a fine brief glimpse they give of a creative force at work. Do not fear the chaos of the mind. Your very universe is astir there, waiting only for the primal signal, "Let there be light!"

WHAT'S NEW?

Thoughts change with the times, but emotions remain fixed. We have tapped old Thomas Hardy for this one. Thoughts about love, for instance, change with the years and eras, but has there been the slightest change in the emotion? The contemporary poet, or any writer for that matter, finds himself dealing with unchangeable feelings in the language and thought of his changing time. What's new under the sun?

❖

It has become something of a commonplace to discourse on Robert Frost's poem, "Stopping By Woods on a Snowy Evening." If you find it difficult to countenance one more comment, blame the poem. It won't let anyone alone, will it?

The first thing you notice about it, ambitious young poets, is that it deals with the most insignificant of events. Stopping to watch snow falling on a patch of woodland is as ordinary as coming down to breakfast. Lesson One: There is more material close at hand than you'll ever live to finish writing about. If you put the ordinary to work in your creative mind, and let it have its way, it may very well shape itself into something fresh and interesting, even profound. You have to relax and let it act upon you, as we shall explain in Lesson Two:

If Frost actually did stop by those woods and watch that snow, then the very act drew him into a mood which in turn generated the poem. Expressing himself in gifted yet simple language, he ended up speaking "between the lines," and speaking between the lines is one of the impressive techniques of poetry. It goes far beyond the ability to describe accurately—itself no mean feat. It fashions the unusual from the usual. A poem that says something by suggestion, instead of straight out, has achieved a special kind of success. In the case of this particular one, by the time you get to the last two lines, that masterful bit of repetition, you are stopped in your tracks and caused to meditate. Taking hold of the reader from within like that, making him think for think for himself, is the supreme art. Happy indeed is the poet who can produce a few stanzas that won't leave anybody alone.

❖

Here's a small point—trivial perhaps, but likely to annoy some editors. Effective as it may be to have one of your characters "hiss" a remark, you should first make sure you put a sibilant or two into the remark. "Oh, I hate you!" she hissed. This is a no-no simply because it is impossible to hiss such a phrase. Yet you'll find this sort of thing turning up not infrequently even in published fiction. "You stinking so-and-so" would at least have some sonics going for it. It would make an authentic hiss. Along similar lines, remember that a remark cannot be "smiled." "I like you," he smiled. A smile, though, is wordless in actual practice. The way to combine words and smiles is simply to separate them. "I like you." He smiled. Or, "I like you," he said, smiling. Don't play loose with language. Every care you can take with it is worth the effort.

❖

The outward appearance of dawdling often gives creativity a bad name. Why are you lolling in that chair or strolling from window to window? Why aren't you *doing* something? Before you begin booting yourself into action, biting your nails, consider the possibility that you have merely been temporarily deactivated while some creative action is going on deep down inside you. Are you out of sorts, or are you in good spirits? The former results in lethargy, the latter in awareness. Tune your inner ear to the voices that may be waiting to speak. Mozart composed that way. He reported when he was in good spirits, and apparently idling, he found the ideas flowing.

❖

There is a fine line, by the way, between dawdling and getting to work. You'll have to learn to tread that fine line. The two are not necessarily in conflict. Suddenly possessed by an idea, your whole being may be deathly quiet in response. When it is time to try the idea out in words, you'll get the signal.

EXHIBIT "A"

What is the mystery of the single shoe, and why does it keep turning up from time to time? On a city street, or a highway, or down a lane, every so often you will come across it lying there waiting to be questioned. It may very well be waiting for the approach of a writer. The more sensitive the writer, the more likely he or she will be to pose the questions.

How did it get there? Who lost it, if indeed it was actually lost? If it wasn't lost, why was it discarded? What did the wearer do, if anything, about it? (Hah, you see? We have progressed at once from the object to thoughts about people, characters.)

If you are a writer at heart, don't leave this page without jotting down six people who might possibly have owned it, six reasons why they lost it, or left it, or didn't come looking for it, and six sequences which, combined with the above, might be initial springboards for a short story. Carry your favorite of these springboards around with you for a few hours, then sit down and have a try at writing the story, say in a thousand or two thousand words. Masterpiece or disposable junk, you will have given yourself a complete writing experience. Don't worry if you discover that you aren't Timothy Findley. There may have been a time when he couldn't write, either.

Do you take advantage of those periods when, for no apparent reason, you are on top of the world, elated, raring to go? Learn to recognize such a state as a creative state. It is during that soaring of the emotions that you might very well seize a sheet of paper and write whatever comes, irrelevant, crazy, verbose as it may be. Write unrestrained until the whole expression begins to slow down. What is there before you on the paper may surprise you. You can pick out what you want, and shape it up, afterwards. If you think there is nothing there at all, evaluate it again. What is there in your very nature that might have sparked it? No creative outburst can be totally without significance.

❖

Be sure you are aware of, and have respect for, the rules and forms of the language. You learned the rules of grammar in your school days. Later on in your writing career you may decide to ease a few of them out the window. but in some strange way your writing will be at its most effective if you have learned them thoroughly first. Think of them not as shackles but rather as vehicles of expression. Johann Sebastian Bach found some of his greatest freedom while constructing his incomparable examples of the fugue, than which there is no stricter musical form. Mozart, for all his apparently spontaneous masterpieces, was in fact an industrious student. He said himself there wasn't a great composer whose works he had not studied thoroughly.

The poet who can write an acceptable sonnet or villanelle is quite likely to show a measure of control over his free verse as well. You can't set rules aside if there are no rules, can you?

❖

What is your poem saying that will make the reader want to read it again? Are you pricking him with some new insight, or are you merely repeating what he could say for himself? Can you present the reader with a little something he ought to have thought of but didn't? Can you be your original self and not a glorified copyist?

❖

Can you write a summary of your story in once sentence? A somewhat stringent test, to be sure, but at least it will show whether you have been moving forward towards an outcome and not just standing around talking.

DREAM UP

We have all had, many times perhaps, a ridiculous dream; a dream so absurd, so irrelevant, making so little sense, that we pass it off as unexplainable fantasy. We may tell it to someone the next day and then let forgetfulness carry it away into that outer space where all things forgotten go. Now, let's not take our book of ten thousand dreams down from the shelves, or our revised Freud either. Whatever those French poodles were doing worrying at the heels of orange pickers in the Yukon, or why we had to jump off a departing freight train which had suddenly picked up speed at an alarming rate, only to find that it was in reality an ocean liner and we were now floundering in the sea with marine lights fading into the distance, the fact remains that it was our own particular dream. (Take a breath.) As creative writers, might we not have a try at putting it to our own particular use?

Instead of telling your dream at all, instead of writing it out in full and filing it uselessly away, try this. Make a list of all the chief nouns that turned up in it. Then make a list of all the action verbs. Pick out half a dozen nouns and half a dozen verbs that seem to catch your fancy for no immediate reason. Study this list and cut it down by half. Carry this concentrated list in your mind all day, or in your pocket, and stay alert in case you get any messages. What are you doing here, playing games? Sure. We don't speak of the "writing game" for nothing.

❖

The opening line of "East Coker", the second of T.S. Eliot's *Four Quartets*, reads:

In my beginning is my end.

That might very well have been spoken by the genius, the essential spirit, of the short story. It has been said that the end of a short story should be implicit in its beginning. Think that over. Think of any short story that you have read and admired. Think of its opening passage.

43

Does it somehow seem to foreshadow its ending? Or, if you find that too tough to manage, is the ending in agreement with the material set forth, disclosed to the reader, at the outset? A story that moves from here to there, with no distracting bypaths to lead the reader off somewhere else, is a story that fulfills its narrative requirement. It is of a piece. It will stand complete in the memory.

Why do writers in a creative mood so often speak of rolling a sheet of paper into the typewriter? Don't they know they should always roll in two sheets? It helps protect the roller, the platen. It sounds better, too, that slight bit of padding.

To write short stories, or poems, you have to use your imagination – a crashing banality that will startle no one. Don't forget, though, that your reader has an imagination too. Give him a couple of elements which, when put together, will engender a surprise, or a realization, and you have him hooked. A simple example of this is the haiku form, that deceptive little three-line poem which acts directly upon the imagination of the reader. It is a general rule of haiku that the poet must not say anything poetic. (Another surprise?) The fact is that it is the reader who is expected to be poetic. He becomes, in a way, himself the poet when he puts together in his mind the simple ingredients the original poet has given to him.

> In the dark root house
> Potatoes dry in the bins;
> the earthy odour. *J.V.H.*

> Thunder in the south:
> hollyhock to hollyhock
> the hummingbird darts. *J.V.H.*

This little spark-gap in the reader's imagination might well be noted by the fiction writer too. Don't insist on telling the readers what they might enjoy realizing for themselves.

GIVING THE GEARS

Beginning a story with a snatch of dialogue is sometimes a good idea. It is inviting. An exchange of talk between a couple of characters is easy to read. The very look of it on the page is conducive to giving it a run-through, and the reader is drawn into the story before he realizes it.

Warning Sign: If you begin with dialogue, the reader will at once start to imagine the characters in his mind. He can hardly help it. Therefore, you must somehow contrive to make the reader imagine the right characters. Consider this:

"Hello, is that you?"
"Who else?"
"I just got that letter from Chris."
"It's about time. What's the news?"

Any reader would be willing to go on from there, but note that he would go on with no information as to the sex of the characters or what sort of characters are speaking. It might be two men, two women, a fellow and his girl friend, a mother telling her husband at the office that a letter had just arrived from their son, or daughter. Whatever the reader has in mind by now, he'll have to change gears and start all over again if he discovers a few sentences later that the characters are entirely different from those he had half imagined. The reader should be given at least an inkling. Let's try this:

"Hello, Jim?"
"Who else, sweety-girl?"
"I just got that letter from Christine."
"Can't wait to read it. Can I pick you up for lunch?"

You have now pointed the reader in the right direction. You have established the sex of the characters, their relationship is suggested, and perhaps their general age range – all this in the first five words. Never confuse readers by causing them to stall and have to change those gears we mentioned. Send them on their way from the proper starting point.

Speaking of sex change, which in a way we were, there is a somewhat similar problem when you write a story in the first person. If the sex of your first person character is opposite to that of the author, whose name (yours) appears at the head of the piece, be sure you tip the reader off right away. If a story, for instance, is by Sally Jane Grubero, and the first sentence is "I was sitting in my easy chair looking over..." the reader may very well assume that the narrator is a woman. At least, this reader (who admittedly may not be oversharp) always does. What an ordeal of gear-changing to discover on page two that the "I" is a man. If so, this could have been easily indicated by beginning the story, "I was sitting in my easy chair packing my pipe...". The smallest bit of information may be all that is needed to get the reader off on the right track.

❖

It can't be repeated too often that nouns and verbs are the very stuff of effective language. They form the spinal column of a good sentence or a good poetic line. Adjectives and adverbs can be done without unless they are precise, unless they answer a need that can't be fulfilled otherwise. Then they shine. Don't let them offer their services indiscriminately. Make them wait until they are wanted. If one of your characters is seen running swiftly down the street, he'll be even more alive and visible if he *races* down the street. The right verb may not need qualifying. Your fiery red sunset might be more interesting if it appeared as Valhalla burning; and you'd be replacing the two adjectives with an effective metaphor.

❖

Everyone who writes, and everyone who doesn't, should own a copy of Fowler's *Modern English Usage*. It is so much more than a book of rules. It is sheer good reading, and entertainment for any lively mind. Incidentally, what better way of killing off an occasional attack (real or imagined) of Writer's Block?

NO DENYING

Most writers know quite well that coincidence is unacceptable as a solution to a fictional problem or predicament. If a main character, after a series of ever worsening situations, finally has his back to the wall and is about to be evicted from his apartment because his overdue rent has piled up to here, and if the day before his eviction the mail brings him a cheque for two thousand dollars as a birthday present from a rich uncle he'd forgotten he had, that simply won't do as a solution to his immediate problem. It won't do because the author has run himself out of invention and has dragged in aid to which he is not entitled.

Note, though, that if the same bit of coincidence appears at the opening of the story, the reader can do nothing but accept it. There can be no denying that it happened. It is a fact he has no way of disputing. He must read on in order to find out what the author is going to do with it, what story is to come of it.

If you want to write a story based on a wild coincidence, fine — as long as the coincidence appears right away and is indeed the story's basis. If he wished to make use of that masterly concoction about the overdue rent, we might begin the yarn like this:

> When I slit open uncle Fred's letter and found the two-thousand dollar cheque, on the very eve of my eviction for arrears of rent, I leaned against the wall for support while the other walls began to swim.

That, mark you, is not the story. The story takes off with that incident. There will be more to it than our hero's financial difficulties. The coincidence will be what brought on the whole thing.

Can you think up half a dozen coincidences, not quite so silly, each of which you might use as the springboard, the jumping-off point, for a story?

❖

One of W.H. Auden's poems begins:

> My dear one is mine as mirrors are lonely

For years, in my mind, that line has been quietly insisting that it is one of the loveliest lines in our literature. I am not prepared to rear up and argue that it is. I know only what it does to me. And I know that one of the most important aspects of poetry is its *effect*. Get out your scalpel, carve the Auden line into small pieces, pick it apart, go into a trance with simile, metaphor, create mental pictures as you will; the chances are you will never quite isolate or define the essential *effect*. Poetry is like that. You are never done with it when you (think you) have discovered what it *means*. It is your blood that knows what it means.

❖

Marianne Moore speaks of "elephants with their fog-coloured skin." When you find an adjective like that, you have found the reason for adjectives. Will you ever look at an elephant in quite the same way again?

❖

Could you paint a sharp word-picture of crippling old age without using a single adjective? Listen to Yeats:

> Sound of a stick upon the floor, a sound
> From somebody that toils from chair to chair.

Two lines. Five nouns. One verb so accurate that it literally lights up the screen.

❖

Robert Frost said that a poem begins with a lump in the throat. Now, don't get carried away and assume he was referring to a violent surge of emotion. Nevertheless, the mechanism that was triggered is the same. Where may your hand be likely to go on hearing a piece of news that concerns you personally? To your throat. The first stirring of a poem is a piece of news. It is your own "throat reaction" that will take over from there. A dozen small influences will move in and fasten themselves around it, and you will be caught up, involved in the process of composition.

48

WHAT IS TRUTH?

Here's a long-ago phrase from Lorna Crozier, whether or not she even remembers saying it:

Writers are always fabricating.

I know a woman who comes from an uncommonly strict ethnic background. She does some writing, and once she reported that her background people, at least the elders in it, would not countenance fiction. If something was not true, then it was a lie and should not be propagated.

Few writers will take a thing like that too seriously. It does, however, put the finger on us in one respect. We are reporting something that is not true, that never happened, and we ask the reader to believe it. Our problem then is to sell the fabrication to the reader. Let's extract from this bit of nonsense a fundamental truth about writing:

Your story will die on the page if the reader treats it so casually as to regard it as merely putting him on, telling him something that isn't true anyway and therefore doesn't matter much. Your story will come alive if the reader can be so drawn into it that he is in effect living through the experience himself. If he is there on the spot and watching it happen, or better still becoming the main character to whom all these things are happening, he can do nothing but believe it. You might say the essence of the art of fiction writing is the clothing of falsehood in the garments of truth.

A man famous in history once asked, "What is truth?" Writers know.

❖

No doubt the fiction writer's favourite words are "The End." To be able to write them at the bottom of the first draft of a novel, or at the finish of a lengthy short story, is conducive to a comfortable sigh of relief. Don't let those two little words fool you, though. What you might very well have written is "The Beginning." You have enjoyed ridding yourself of all those words; you have enjoyed living with all those fascinating characters all this time; but now the work, as opposed to the creation, starts. Have you the stamina to revise, to refine, to readjust scenes, to write some of them over again if necessary? One author said novels are not written—they are rewritten. Someone else said you never finish a novel—you abandon it. Much the same has been said of a poem. That is to say, there is apparently no end to the chore of finally making the thing the very best you can accomplish. A regular contributor to the old *Collier's* magazine once confessed privately that the published version of a particular short story of his represented the eighteenth revision. The publishers themselves never knew the extent of his labours. The "writing is work" phrase is echoed by established writers everywhere.

It has been said that time is nature's way of preventing everything from happening at once. At first glance this seems to be no more than a humorous remark. If you dwell on it for a few moments, though, you begin to see an underlying truth—a sort of scientific truth. Is humour your particular field of writing? If so, keep an ear cocked for a truth moving below the surface. Some of the best humour conspires to point up a continuing human foible of some sort. How often have you heard a joke and then said, "How true!" Slapstick is all very well, but there is also a ready audience for humour that somehow spades up our deficiencies and brings them into the light for a laugh. Remember Stephen Leacock?

Public approval of a work of art is gravy—a pleasant bonus after the fact. The artist (writer, painter, sculptor, whatever) dare not set out to please in advance. He must produce his work because he is driven to relieve himself of it, to ease the tension that is gripping him. Should he find the public pouring out its approval afterwards, he will have earned the broad smiles that massage his cheek bones.

FRONT ROW

A one-paragraph crash course in getting a story started. Light the lights on your mental stage and sit down in one of the front rows. Wait there in silence until a character walks on. Notice in detail his or her appearance, movements, mannerisms, emotional condition. Keep quite still. Watch for a second character to appear, perhaps two or three. Give them the same treatment. Listen for the first spoken word, the first exchange of words. Don't leave your seat — they must not know you are there. At the first move you make they may scuttle off stage and you'll never see them again. If you can stand this much concentration, they will begin little by little to tell you their story. They will indicate to you what's up, what expectations there are of its progression, perhaps even suggest how it is all likely to end. You daren't assume the role of director until you have the kernel of it firmly in hand. Even then, be careful. You didn't invent this thing. They did. You are merely on hand to record it. At least, it is just that kind of patient approach that will help make you a writer.

If one of your story characters enters his assigned hotel room and finds a bit of plaster fallen from the ceiling, and a cracked window pane patched with a strip of masking tape, you won't have to tell your reader that it is a pretty cheap joint. Add a chipped wash basin and a circle of scale formed around the outlet, and the whole picture comes alive in the reader's mind. When you are describing a setting, remember that you need not talk to the reader directly. Give your readers one or two relevant details through the eyes of one of your characters and leave them to construct the whole scene for themselves. They'll do it gladly. One may not see exactly the same picture as some other, but it will be sharp because it is personal. There is such a thing as creative reading.

❖

Herrick's poem "Upon Julia's Clothes" begins like this:

Whenas in silks my Julia goes,
Then, then, methinks, how sweetly flows
That liquefaction of her clothes.

No, you wouldn't write a poem like that today, but what a fine example of one of poetry's particular attributes, delight — sheer delight as expressed in words. Julia rustles as she walks, apparently. No one but a poet would think of her sound as becoming liquid in the ear. The poetic mind hovers just above the straight line of day-to-day speech. Julia rustling as she walks is a charming idea; the liquefaction turns it into poetry. You can almost taste it, can't you?

❖

In very early centuries church bells were often rung to ward off evil spirits and demons. These wicked entities were wont to hover over the roof tops, and they fled at the sound of the bells. Bells have tongues. They speak a language of their own. How effective creative writing is in dispersing the evil spirits of depression, discontent, melancholy. Robert Louis Stevenson said, "Bright is the ring of words / When the right man rings them."

Those few jumbled sentences have been left in their disconnected state on purpose, as material for a few minutes' meditation. Let them wander through your mind. Put them in sequence for yourself. Make of them what you will.

❖

Learn to write with the whole body. The mind should not be a slave driver, forcing the fingers to answer its every command. Wield your pen, or strike your typewriter keys, with freedom. Let the fingers cooperate. Let them, too, feel the exhilaration of the creative process. Cramped fingers, who knows, may provoke colourless words. Approach the whole matter, if you will, like a deep breathing exercise. Allow the joy of it to circulate. Well-being is a physical thing too. If your back hurts, something's wrong.

SEE ME

Are all novels autobiographical? Perhaps the question is too blatant. It is like asking an author if he bases his characters on real people. If you ask him this he may at once shy away from it, fearing to admit that he might be any sort of gossip monger. That he snoops and makes money out of it. Fearing lest he get himself involved in lawsuits.

Observation of people is in very truth a large part of the novelist's technique. He does not transfer them to manuscript as they are, however, but as he sees them through his own eyes. He may deliberately bring bits of their personalities to the fore, and suppress other bits. In other words, he remodels them as necessary, to suit his purpose of the moment. At his best, he becomes in a way the characters he is writing about. When he does this, his characters are authentic because he is infusing them with himself. Perhaps the author-credit on a book jacket or on a spine should read, for instance: By David Carpenter himself. (Name picked at random, Dave.)

Inarguably, a bit of the author is in every character in his book. All characters, if they are alive and kicking, are having a shot at autobiographies. This is not to say, certainly, that the novelist is really divulging a part of his life story. When he goes about his business of observing characters, though, to what degree is he observing himself? We are all aware that every writer is putting himself on paper for the world to see. If you fear to put yourself on paper, you refrain from writing.

❖

A poem may keep you guessing and yet be clear enough. To carry the implication of this forward, perhaps the *meaning* of a poem should not be the first avenue of investigation. Had the poet wanted to hand the reader a definite *meaning*, he might have been better advised to put it into light verse or even into prose. There is evidently more going on in a poem than literal meaning. The sensual attraction of refined language is a moody thing, and the creation of mood is a very real part of the practice of poetry. In an unrestrained moment one might go overboard and say it is the whole thing, but let's rein up just short of that. Certainly what the poet is trying to do is create in the reader the mood he is in himself. If he succeeds, then what he is saying will be perceived by the sense rather than by the mind. We seem to know certain things intuitively, don't we? We don't expect to pick them apart and prove them in prose sentences. The poet is, in a way, saying what he knows in his bones. Before the reader begins to fidget over what a poem means, he should first allow it to entrance him. When the poet's mood has reached out and enfolded him, perhaps he will begin to sense as the poet senses. People who complain that they can't understand poetry might be very well asked to stop probing and just listen.

❖

You will hear people say from time to time—people who think they'd like to write but probably never will—that they have "great ideas" in their heads for stories but can't put them on paper. Maybe they are just kidding themselves. How do they know they have great ideas if they have never set any of them down where they can see them? Having great ideas is no credit to anyone unless they, the ideas, can be used, put to work. A thorough knowledge of language might quite possibly start them working.

❖

Perhaps there are as many reasons for writing as there are writers. The wish to do anything at all may be engendered by any number of the most personal proddings. The "I can do it too" reason for writing is commendable, as long as one realizes that the road ahead may be long and difficult. If the wish is strong enough, that is no obstacle. A healthy response to initial failure will be, "I can't do it yet, but." In ferreting out the real reason for writing, psychiatrist Edmund Bergler came to the conclusion that a writer stands accused before an invisible jury, and his defence is to write.

Hang that one one your wall. It just might be worth looking at every morning.

WHERES AND WONDERS

One of the great clichés of the writing game is this, that ideas are everywhere. It may take years, though, for the truth of this to sink in. The problem is not to produce an idea, but to put one to work. When, in any humdrum sequence of events, or in any half hour's reading, a particularly appealing word or phrase detaches and comes at you, pick it out of the air and write it down. Write it down and begin playing with it. Playing around is a vice for writers to cultivate. You do not need the great idea. The slightest and most irrelevant germ is capable of breeding. Where the germ came from has little or no significance. The mind is a breeding ground. *A loaf from the crumbs of history.* There's a random and irrelevant phrase for you. It popped into my mind at this very moment, I swear. Where would you take it?

Where did you go last summer, last winter, whenever? Did you at any time find yourself in strange surroundings, a new and different place? Did you spend ten minutes brooding over it, wondering just what type of story or poem might arise from it? If you never saw the place before, it ought to have set your writer's mind speculating. Most literary works, large or small, begin with feeling. Strange places can generate strange feelings. In short, don't ever neglect locale as profitable source material. The beauty of locale is that it will often suggest its own material if you give it a chance – the very opposite of going about feverishly hunting for ideas.

I saw a forlorn-looking little old man, bedraggled, eighty if he was a day, standing at a counter carefully filling out a sweepstake form. And I wondered, what would he do with a sudden avalanche of a million dollars, or four million, or seven? And what plans might potential predators make if they found out? And might the insignificant little old

55

man prove to be a lot smarter than we thought? *And I wondered* is a tool of the writer's trade. How many times have you used it lately?

❖

If all you see in a ball game is a string of fellows taking turns trying to hit a ball, and sometimes succeeding, you are getting some pretty casual entertainment. On the other hand if you see a dangerous base runner streaking it successfully to second, with a known power hitter coming up next; if you feel the tension crackling between pitcher and batter as the one readies his deciding pitch and the other stands poised to smash it over the wall; if you see a fielder snatch a ball hot off the ground with two choices where to throw it; if you note the manager pacing the dugout with seconds left in which to decide on his next strategy; then you are involved in the game and your heart is beating time to the excitement.

Readers of fiction are getting entertainment. When a writer reads fiction he finds himself involved in its execution, noting how the author gets his effects; how he feeds in information without handing it to the reader direct; how skillfully he withholds information so that the reader will not have it too soon; how he sparks a phrase with just the right word; how he is able to lead the reader up a blind alley without in any way cheating him; how he makes the reader set up tensions for himself; how he demonstrates the general craft of the game. I knew a writer who complained that he could no longer read stories for entertainment—he was too busy watching the wheels go round. An extreme case, perhaps, but you get the idea. When you read like that, you are giving yourself something very like a course in writing.

HAVE A GOOD DAY

When someone asks you why you write, don't be afraid to reply, "For fun." The four and twenty elders of the Apocalypse, referring to all created things, said "and for thy pleasure they are and were created." Fanciful or factual as you may prefer, that is just one more Biblical statement from which writers may extract a truth, to wit, creating for pleasure is all the reason one needs.

The fondest hope of the creative artist is that this pleasure might go on to the end of his life. One of the great examples in history is that of Johann Sebastian Bach, who, on his deathbed and already blind, dictated his last composition, one more chorale prelude for the organ, to his son-in-law.

Why did he do this? He couldn't help it, that's why. The act of writing music was as natural to him as that of breathing, and they both stopped together. He died, in fact, in the very act. Just a few bars before the end of the work he breathed his last. The son-in-law, fully conversant with the great man's style and technique, filled in the final short passage himself.

How splendid a thing that death should call a halt to *activity*. That he should not find one sitting waiting for the lifting of the latch.

❖

If you set out to write a story, or a poem, with a shocker ending, be sure you don't dissipate the shock by supplying the reader with unnecessary wordage. A good example of this is in Housman's grim little poem, "Eight O'clock". A condemned man is to be hanged at exactly eight o'clock. There he stands on the trap, bound, waiting. He hears the town clock going through the four quarter chimes that precede the eight o'clock strike. (A bit stark, but this was many years ago.) The poem ends thus:

> Strapped, noosed, nighing his hour,
> He stood and counted them and cursed his luck;
> And then the clock collected in the tower
> Its strength, and struck.

And what happens to you, the reader? You can literally see the wretched fellow dropping through the trap. You can almost hear the snap as the rope jerks taut. Now, if the ending had stated that the clock struck and he plunged through the trap to his death, the whole effect would have been spoiled. As it is, the required picture is painted on the reader's imagination.

The reader's imagination is a very real part of a writer's equipment. Take advantage of it, as often as you can.

❖

What to do with people who can't spell. Writers have a responsibility to the language. They are its guardians, and when any of their friends are obviously off the track they should help them back on. One particular problem, rife nowadays, will be readily recognized in the following solution to it.

Bid your friends write three words on a blackboard, if they have one, or on the kitchen wall, or anywhere:

> his
> hers
> its

Tell them these are all possessives: belonging to him, belonging to her, belonging to it. Then have them write down three more:

> he's
> she's
> it's

Tell them these are all contractions — that is to say, a letter has been left out: he is, she is, it is.

We have hardly touched on the use of the apostrophe here, but one thing at a time. You might want to drop a friendly hint, though, that *shirt's* and *shoe's* are not plurals. By what mental contortion did that apostrophe ever get in there? (As get in it did, right in a store window.) Perhaps a second hint that when you want to make a word possessive you should first write the word down. *Write it down.* Then you proceed to make it possessive, but you don't monkey with the word. You write it down and leave it there. This will easily avoid referring to such things as a *boy's choir*, which would mean a choir belonging to a boy instead of composed of *boys*. Writers, be teachers!

HEART OF THE MATTER

Tension causes high blood pressure, strokes, heart attacks, death. It also causes entertainment, exhilaration, life. It causes writers. Relief of tension is, in a way, the gist of fiction. The opening of a story should present a situation that ought to be adjusted, relieved, brought to a conclusion, not left to lie as it is. The reader's interest will be in seeing the strings drawn together. What is going to happen that will really matter? What will it all come to? Something is out of whack here; what series of events will straighten it out? The straightening out, by the way, need not be achieved by overt action. It may be an inner growth or change in a certain character's outlook or point of view. There may be a moral decision to be made. But the reader should know at the end that the tension is over, that the spring has been released, and that what happened in the narrative was logical and right.

❖

Once, at an office supply sale, I came upon a big display of white bond paper at a bargain price. It seemed such a good deal that I bought several hundred sheets, thinking I might just as well use it for random writing instead of the familiar yellow newsprint known in the trade as canary news. Before long I was surprised to find that it wasn't working. I couldn't use it for the purpose. White bond, no matter how cheap, was for finished copy, not for first drafts or for initial fiddlings. I gave up and went back to the old canary news. Creativity was pale yellow in colour.

This shot me into big company as I recalled that Kipling had to have paper in a shade of off-white blue. (He also had to grind his own ink powder.) Schiller's rotten apples are now well known – he kept one in his desk because the odour inspired him to create. There are numerous other crackpot examples even among our contemporaries.

If you have some idiosyncrasy which you associate directly with creative activity, don't try to sneer it away. Cultivate it. No one need know. Who's to complain, unless of course the smells get out of hand. Why do some first-rate novelists write on the kitchen table? If that's what your imp requires before he'll deliver, let him have it. It may be part of the whole unexplainable scheme of things. Try writing in a big empty room. Try writing in a closet. Try anything you like, but get words on paper. That, as they say, is the bottom line.

❖

If the characters in your story are camera-clear in your mind to begin with, you won't have to go back over the script and check whether you have allowed the colour of their hair or their eyes, or their height, or anything else about them, to change somewhere in mid-stream.

❖

The freedom in free verse is not a freedom to wander. Not a freedom to relax. Not a freedom to be aimless. Not a freedom to dispense with all rhythm and form. Not a freedom to write a long prose sentence and proceed to chop it up into short pieces and set them one on top of the other. Perhaps it isn't freedom at all. A river looks as though it was originally free to wind and wander where it pleased, but this was not so. It was directed by forces that turned it relentlessly this way and that. The basis of music is rhythm, its driving force. The basis of poetry is the same. A poetic insistence must control your free verse. At its best it will have a sort of race memory of its beginnings, of being turned in new directions, of singing instead of speaking, of thought guided into some new level of expression.

HOW AND HOW NOT

One "how to write a novel" idea of some years ago went like this. You write the outline of your story in about five hundred words, a couple of sheets of double-space typing. Then you take a pencil and arbitrarily mark twenty spots which might represent the beginning of a chapter. Then you supply yourself with twenty sheets of paper and expand the whole thing into twenty chapter outlines. Then (don't forget this) you write the novel.

This is still an attractive scheme, perhaps. The danger is that it may stifle the very creation it seeks to induce. You will by now have a group of characters moving about, and you know what is likely to happen when you try to tell a bunch of characters what to do, don't you? In the actual writing, you may find one or more of them balking, telling you that *you* are not following *their* direction. It's the old subconscious at work. Writing itself is largely unconscious, largely the process of the mind working at a deeper level than you realize. At its best, it will hand you little creative pieces as you need them. Try and tell it in advance just what you are going to do, and it may turn two deaf ears.

Don't disparage the outline, though. You might feel inspired, just producing a synopsis and then expanding it. Perhaps it wouldn't be such a bad idea to write such an outline, and then throw it in the fireplace some cozy frosty evening and pull up a typewriter and begin writing the novel. If there were any characters lurking in the shadows waiting to be used, they'd smile.

❖

Own up. Have you ever sat down and read the introduction to, say, the *Concise Oxford Dictionary*? Twenty pages of explanatory talk, by and large about language. What is a writer's chief concern? Language.

❖

A useful assignment would be to jot down half a dozen familiar words and then write a concise definition of each. A dictionary definition, if you

61

like. Could you, for instance, explain *cat* in five words? Try *sensible*, in three separate applications. *Derivative, camp, kiss.* Useful, did we say? A little exercise in achieving compression, terseness, marks of the competent writer. You could lose a reader in a hundred words when you might have grabbed him in fifty.

❖

"Write about what you know" is a piece of advice given continually to writers. It has become a basic rule. Truth, in writing, stems from the simple fact that you know what you are talking about because you have experienced it. Nothing will show up falsity faster than the suspicion that the writer is just guessing. Guessing at the locale he is setting his story in, for instance. Guessing about the game he is describing. Guessing at how a particular business is run. Guessing at music. Falsity will quickly shy a reader off.

In absorbing the "know" rule, however, it is well to remember that it doesn't matter how you know. You may not know a particular setting or subject first hand, but if your interest in it is keen enough you will have absorbed every bit of information about it that you can lay your hands on. You will investigate to the core. If you weren't present at the Battle of Hastings, but you wish to do a yarn set in 1066, you will begin by lapping up a shelfful of information about the life and manners of that period. You will become an authority on your subject. You will be able to prove a point, if necessary, as though from personal experience. It is difficult to argue against thorough research.

Writing about what you know has these two aspects. They come together nicely for a writer who takes his job seriously.

I WISH AND I WISH

Wishful thinkers have no place in the writing game. How often have you heard one of them say, "If only I had (or could get) an idea." What they really mean is, "If only I could find a complete story, all ready to write." Such a thing has indeed been known to happen, but the odds against it are astronomical. And there are grave doubts that it has ever happened to a beginner. If you wait for it you will quite possibly never write at all.

Take the slightest idea. Take a single word. Reflect on it. (This is the proper application of dreaming.) Let every association you can think of cling to it. It can do nothing but grow.

How does that quotation go? 'The kingdom of heaven is like leaven, which a woman took, and hid in three measures of meal, till the whole was leavened.' Substitute *writing* for *the kingdom of heaven*, and you've got it.

A stunt practised from time to time by some writers' groups is to sit in a circle, pick someone to "start a story," and let the story grow from person to person as it travels round the ring. This is all very well, on a see-what-will-happen basis, as long as there is a general sense of where the story is headed. If allowed to run wild, it can end up in a hodge-podge going nowhere in all directions. So be careful. Perhaps it would be logical to establish first the field, the limits in which the story will operate, the general direction it is to take, and what it should come to. There is nothing like a sense of ending to draw a yarn relentlessly towards the finish line.

It comes close to being a rule, for beginners to follow, that you should know the ending before you begin. To keep you on track there is absolutely nothing like an end in sight. Put it in ten words and hang it on the wall. Whenever a bright idea strikes in the course of the writing, read the writing on the wall and make sure the two are in harmony. Some famous writers have said that they do not themselves know the ending until they get there, but you may have to write a dozen novels to develop any skill in that kind of sleight-of-hand.

❖

If an incident, or a phrase, or an apt bit of description, stays in your mind and won't let you forget it, if it recurs from time to time as sharp as ever, that's a sure sign that it contains material you could use. It is the subconscious keeping in touch, throwing an occasional signal. Sooner or later you'll get the go-ahead. It will be time then to sit down and begin to write.

❖

Don't be in a hurry to discard an apparent failure. Put it away for awhile. Let it rest. Three months later, or six, reading it again after it has cooled, you may very well find out what to do with it. You may get a new insight, see a new angle. The subconscious will have been working away at it on your behalf. This is precisely how that mind operates. It will often solve a problem for you by itself, if you don't keep disturbing it by trying to think!

❖

Think of your poem as an investigation. There is investigation with the microscope; there is investigation into limitless space. Poetry is investigation of the spirit. If a poem you read moves you, something must have happened. Perhaps it told you something you didn't know, which indeed smacks somewhat of prose. Perhaps it told you something you had forgotten you knew, which is closer to poetry. But if it stirred in you an awareness that left your senses glowing, and your body with them, then it was poetry for its own sake. It investigated you. It did its job.

THE ODD THING IS

One morning at spring breakup time a tombstone, still standing, came floating down the North Saskatchewan River on a block of ice. An alert Prince Albert photographer snapped it, and the picture appeared in the press. An oddity of any kind is good subject matter. Whenever you witness, or hear about, an oddity, make a note of it in your writer's scrapbook.

Some writers have difficulty moving characters around. They think that unless the reader sees a character setting one foot down after the other, all the way, that character won't be a visible reality. Oddly enough, this is not so. Your reader is quite capable of taking little mental steps, and he will enjoy doing it. Petey, say, has been watching something from a window on the other side of the room, and is now over at her desk answering the phone. When she hangs up, perhaps frowning, are you then faced with the problem of tracing her course back to the window so that she can be seen moving? Not at all. You simply continue, "Back at the window, she frowned at..." If this seems a stupid example, be assured that some writers are actually bothered by logisitics equally uncomplicated. Or, if you want a complete change of scene, it is often possible simply to move the writing down an extra couple of spaces and begin the new section. The reader will understand quite well that he is somewhere else. Many a problem in writing can be solved by being direct and by trusting your reader to come along with you.

❖

As we said before, editors have definite ideas about what they want, and you have to fit in with these if you want them to publish you. So, why not write and ask them what they want? The surprising answer is that they might not quite know. Their definite ideas are hidden even from them, sometimes, and we have to be satisfied with the fact that all they know for certain is what they *don't* want. They will, however, and without fail, recognize what they want when they see it. Study their publications if you are not already familiar with them, read their market notes in writers' magazines, avoid sending them what they plainly don't fancy, and you'll have a better chance of brightening their eyes with something they can use. That is, if it's something good they can use.

It would seem to be a sound piece of advice never to send a short story, or even a novel, out to market until you are well into occupation with the next one. The exhilaration of the new project will make a fine cushion for rejection, if rejection comes. Also, it will help you cast a cool editorial eye over the returned item. Was it the best I could do? Should I just send it out again, or could it use some further attention? One way or another, there is nothing like work in progress to keep one's spirits up, one's lamp burning.

Let's say it again. Consciously seeking to curtail adjectives and adverbs in your script, allowing only the vital ones, letting the weight rest as much as possible on nouns and verbs, will not only strengthen your writing but will make the ones you use more vivid. Odd, but true.

❖

A famous last word. If and when you learn to be simple, you will have learned a high truth about writing. Simplicity is top priority. Yeats said it, Hemingway said it, Caldwell said it, and there is similar testimony everywhere. Love of words, yes indeed, but don't get carried away. Love itself is a simple thing. Be simple. Shoulder all those extra words, the ones that are only along for the ride, out of the way. You don't need them. Say it simply. In simplicity is power—write that on your wall too.

ALPHA BETA

A is for *arrest*. You have to arrest the reader's attention. He is not sitting there waiting for you to talk. He will only listen if you obviously have something to say. It may be easy enough to tap him on the shoulder; but when he turns his head you'd better be able to tell him something that will make his eyes light up. Put this on page one, and he's yours. It need not be startling, or shocking; but it should be in some way engrossing. Readers can be fickle. You may only get one chance to arrest their attention.

B is for *banal*. Don't make a song and dance about something everybody knows. Triteness is bad medicine. Your audience may be able to think your great thought for themselves, and think it better. If you are going to tell them what they know already, you must contrive to throw some new light on it, give them some new slant, make them raise their eyebrows and say, "Well, now, I never saw it quite that way before."

C is for *conflict*, one of the key words in fiction. A misunderstood word, too. We hear how necessary conflict is, and we go looking for the standup fight, and we say nuts, nobody would fight over that. Who said anything about fight? The two opposing forces may never openly meet. Consider the head of steam that can build up over "conflict of interests." Wherever something is in disagreement, you have conflict. Wherever something disturbs a normal flow of events, conflict. Conflict is the yes and no of it all, deep down or on the surface as the case may be. Conflict is story. If you have a good conflict going, a plot will appear by itself. It won't have to be constructed. You will only know, after it is all over, what the plot *was*.

D is for *depth*. Depth, great depth, will get you a successful story every time. Perhaps even a powerful story. Depth is not a casual word. It rings the fiction bell, the poetry bell, every writing bell. You'd like it explained? Ask yourself two questions. One, exactly what do you mean when you say someone of your acquaintance has no depth to him? Two, what exactly do you understand by depth of character? Answer these two questions for yourself, and don't let up until your answers are specific and clear to you. You could be giving yourself a mini-course in writing.

E is for *ear*, and this is practically a must. Your must have an ear for words, for language, for its rhythm and flow. Whether you write poetry or fiction, or for that matter non-fiction, your ear will tell you when you are right. There is some doubt that an ear can ever be developed if you don't have a natural one to begin with, but that's putting it at its worst. If you doubt the sensitivity of your writer's ear, try a continuing program of simply reading great writing. Read it until your whole being is soaked in it. Never doubt that an ear can be trained. You might be right.

F is for *frame*. The "frame" story is hard to manage, ancient mariners notwithstanding. Someone recounts a story or an experience to someone else, and they wind up where they began, the story still hanging on the wall like a picture. This is not to disparage the framing, but if you are new at the game you may be better advised just to tell the story, so that the reader becomes part of it.

G is for *general*. The general remark will wash your feet right out from under you. It will lose your reader faster than shouting "fire!" "Isn't love wonderful" is a general remark of the first order; but if you are going to pass that observation on to a reader, you had better make of it a specific instance, zooming in with accurate detail, something that will explode in his consciousness and make him glad he heard about it once more. Detail, living and relevant detail, can always be counted on to hold the reader's interest.

H is for *honest*. Be honest with your reader. See that you give him all the information he is entitled to. Don't spring something on him at the last minute as a substitute for careful planning from the start. If the killer was the girl who delivers the paper, the little vixen should have been a reasonable part, even if a small part, of the story. If our hero has a brother in the Virgin Islands, the brother has no business appearing unheralded just in time to put the story's complications to rights. I knew a judge who claimed he could tell you who the killer (in a who-dunit) was going to be by the end of Chapter One, providing the entire cast was presented in that first chapter. Perhaps a judicial limb like that is not one to go out on, but nevertheless the reader should be supplied with all necessary information, and not only in a who-dunit either.

I is for *intuition*. What you know without knowing how you know. What you sense in your bones. If you get the mental signal that a particular word in a poem or story is not exactly the right one, make a note of it and wait for the right one to appear. You know it is somewhere, and you know it will come. If you sense that a certain character is getting hard to handle, throw the gears into neutral and let him or her tell you what's wrong. If you realize you are saying something that you wouldn't want to be suddenly asked to prove, mark the spot and make a note to assign it as much research as may be needed to get it ironed out. Intuition is a delicate sense. What made you know instinctively that a certain person you met was not one with whom to exchange confidences? Intuitive writing has a special authenticity. It is right because you know it is right, or something is wrong because you know it is wrong.

J is for *juvenile*. Even though you may have no particular interest in writing for youngsters, bear in mind that you were one yourself once. You went through it all. You think you are grown up and done with it, but somewhere deep down in the old subkonk you are a child still. There is fiction or poetic material there that would surprise you. What exactly was your earliest sorrow? What did you find exciting, experiencing it as you did for the first time? What was your first fear? What was your first confrontation with one of your peers? What are you, right now, anyway? You didn't change much, it is commonly believed, after you were seven. Some of the best writers, it is also believed, have a close emotional tie with their childhood. They soaked up any amount of vital material back there when the world was young.

K is for *knowledge*. It is impossible to know too much. This applies to knowledge of your story's characters as much as to life in general. The more intimately you know your characters, the more real they will become on the page, the more they will live in what you write. You may think you don't need all that extra knowledge, irrelevant as it may appear to be to the story you are telling. But you do, and it isn't. With how much more authority are you able to talk about a friend you have known from childhood than about one whom you met last year? It is the same with friends you invent. It is impossible to know too much about them. In some magic way, the reader will accept them as real, their doings as things that actually happened.

L is for *locale*. Where your story is happening is a vital part of the picture. If the reader knows exactly where he is, the whole thing tends to become real. Avoid lengthy descriptions, which are not nearly as effective as a few significant details. 'Something was going on at the top of the palm tree,' for instance, as an opening sentence, would at once begin to suggest a locale of sorts.

M is for *make-believe*. Pretense. You might say all fiction is make-believe. The moment you say it, though, the warning bells begin to ring. Writers must also take the term in a deeper sense. They must *make* the reader *believe*. Make-believe must be, for the moment, truth. A story becomes truth when its characters are alive, are real. A character becomes real when the reader can see him, can hear him speak — and not before.

N is for *name*. The name of the game. The name of this game is entertainment, more or less. If you are tedious you are entertaining only yourself. The reader expects value-for-the-money. You must make him glad that he sat down and gave you his attention. If, tears or smiles, he wouldn't have missed reading it, then you have done your job as entertainer. You are going to have to answer to the reader, always. If you really don't care whether you get read or not, you aren't a real writer. (Any argument there?)

O is for *onward*, to slip for once into the slightly archaic. The word has a get-up-and-go flavour, though, hasn't it? A story must march. It began at the beginning, let's hope, and it must move steadily to the end. You don't stop to pick flowers or give dissertations on unrelated subjects. If a situation has been set up, and some characters are busy working it to its logical conclusion, you stay where the action is. Even the most philosophical narrative is on the move somewhere, its destination being the final and satisfactory making of its point, its effect. You sense when you read it, if it is a good one, that it is going somewhere step by step, and that it will not stop until it arrives there. A deadly story is one that stands still, dawdles. A deadly poem is one that stalls in a welter of words.

P is for *plot*, a small word with which you can scare yourself to death. There is a mistaken belief that a fully-concocted plot is the beginning of any short story or novel. Ask a couple of dozen established writers about plot, and you'll be surprised how many will tell you they either don't know what it means or never think of it when they write. Well, what then? Get yourself a lively character, with a mind of his or her own, better still two lively characters, and put on the harness yourself while *they* take the reins. If you try to do all the driving you may never get where you should be going. But your fully-realized characters will, because they know!

Q is for *QWERTY*. Qwerty hangs out on the third row of your type-writer keys, to be found, that is, Usually In Orhthographic Places. Speaking of inventing names (which we were, weren't we, with a nod to banality?), do you have trouble thinking up names for your characters? Some writers swear they do. Write down your own name in full and see how many names it will suggest to your sparkling mind. If your name is Montmaurency Fairfield Dickinson, you can begin pouring out Monty, Maurice, Nancy, Dick, Nick, Sonny, Phil, and so on to your stalled heart's content. And the word *stalled* suggests that this might be a good game to play during an attack of that largely fictitious affliction, Writer's Block.

R is for *rewrite*. This is what you must never be afraid to do. All too often you aren't finished when you think you are. Novels, stories, poems, etc., seldom fail to undergo extensive revision before the manuscript ever goes off to market. That polished writing by so-and-so, the stuff you admire so much, was almost certainly not slapped down on to the typewriter as you see it. The genuine writer is a polisher. He wants to be admired, even if he'd hesitate to admit it. You don't put a handful of your flowers in a horticultural show. You do some pretty careful selecting. Only the best is worth displaying. It is a fearful thing to say of a piece of writing, "this is my best," but you should be able to say it.

S is for *subconscious*. The unconscious, if you like. Trust it. Don't try to manipulate it, or understand it. Just trust it. It represents the area in which most of your good writing will be done. Bright ideas that just "come to mind" by themselves are being handed up to you from this mystic source, this magic storehouse. Every detail of the life you have lived, every slightest opinion you ever formed, are stored in the memory of this original example of the computer. Something in it will suddenly click with something you see or hear or read today, and without the slightest warning you have something to write about, story, poem, play, whatever. You can't force the magic to work, but you can be ready for it when it strikes. You learn to stay in the receptive state. You keep constantly aware that the least thing may trigger the action, flimsy as the initial indication of it may be.

T is for *theme*. What are you talking about? What does your piece seem to be illustrating? Can you think of a well-known proverb or saying which might somehow attach to it? Could you do it the other way round, take a proverb first and begin casting about for some characters who might enlighten an understanding of it in a few thousand words? If you think of using theme as a starting point, be careful not to preach. Don't seek to impose your opinions on anybody, unless you are mighty sure you can get away with it. But if a reader reads what you've written and then slaps a hand down and says, "Well, isn't that just like life!" you have put theme to effective use.

U is for *unity*. Your story, or indeed your poem, must hold together in one piece. As a unit, if you like. You are out to make an emotional effect of some sort on the reader. Everything must contribute towards producing that effect. Here you have unity of purpose. You are pursuing a relentless course with this one purpose in view. If you know for certain just what effect you wish to make on the reader, your actions and incidents will not deviate from it. If you are sure what you want to do, your characters will co-operate.

V is for *volume*. The book you dream of having just published, sitting there on the shelf for you to point to with all outward modesty. If you are planning a book, don't lose time dreaming about its completion. Dream of its characters and of what action their very characters suggest they might get involved in. Dream of small details about them, of the hundred bits of their biographies that you may never use or need. When you do this you are living their lives with them. The book itself is going to rise out of their lives. Carry a little pack of index cards about with you, and constantly jot down any ideas or fragments that may cross your mind. No need to begin judging their value; just scribble them down. (This could go on and on, but you get the idea, don't you?)

W is for *wonder*. The wonder of it all, of this most stimulating occupation, writing. What ever do people do who don't write? (Writers in ecstasy burst out with this one frequently.) When you write you are involved in a performance of magic, and the magician's wand is in your own hand. You must act as though someone else, unseen, is wielding it, but everybody else will be quite sure it is you. And if you can pass some of this wonder on to readers, they'll come back to see what you are writing next.

X is for *Xerox*. (This is not advertising copy.) "Xerox" has become in the popular mind almost a synonym for "photocopy." Photocopying is one of the wonders of the age. Its abuse can have serious implications. Be careful what you do with it. Are you infringing the Copyright Act? Have you permission to copy what you just copied? People are running up and down every street with copied stuff in their hands. Did you know that indiscriminate copying of music, for instance, is threatening to put publishers out of business? People who wouldn't dream of walking into a music store, watching to make sure nobody was looking, snatching up forty copies of a choral work, and taking it off to choir practice, will calmly borrow a single copy and take it off to their copying machine. Simple theft. Stealing from publisher, from composer, from retailer. If you expect a square deal from your neighbour, see that you hand one out to him.

Y is for *you*. The general subject in all your writing is YOU. You are writing about you. You are presenting you to the world, when you write. The wider your audience spreads, the more you will be spreading you around. Don't write at all if you are afraid of being found out. In writing, all your fond opinions will one by one appear, all your hidden fears will be exposed, your whole background will be painted on a canvas, your failures will be confessed. Pretty grim? There is a brighter side. There is no therapy quite like writing. It is good for you to turn yourself inside out without knowing you are doing it. If something has been strangling you all your life, sitting down and writing about it will relax the hold. You need not do it directly, but by suggestion. Through your characters, perhaps. If you have troubles, hand them over to your typewriter. The good news is that it is possible to pound them (a familiar expression to writers) out of your system.

Z is for *z-z*, the cartoonist's favorite device for indicating sleep. (Are you still awake?) Need it be suggested that a writer should avoid putting the reader to sleep? Short of an actual treatise on insomnia, the essential job of any piece of writing is to alert the reader and keep him in a conscious state, surely. If someone takes your novel to bed and falls asleep at two-thirty a.m., you can hardly be held responsible. But if your reader succumbs after a good meal, with your book dropping *thud* from his grasp, it carries a message with it to the floor. 'Nuff said.

OLD SAW RESHARPENED

A Non-Play In Less Than One Act
by
John V. Hicks

A sparsely furnished kitchen, back door at left rear. A youngish woman in housecoat and bedroom slippers, hair in curlers, sits at a kitchen table at centre, drinking coffee and reading a magazine. The right rear corner of the room is crudely curtained off with a sheet which slides on curtain rings and wire. A sound of spasmodic typing comes from somewhere not at once apparent. There is a loud knocking on the back door. The woman fastens her housecoat closer as she shuffles off to answer it. Three visitors enter, flinging the door open just before she gets there.

FIRST VISITOR (*a swarthy fellow in walking shorts and shoes*) We want to see Peter Munbrane.

SECOND VISITOR (*a thin girl in jeans, with straggling black hair which partly conceals her face*) You're his wife, hey?

WIFE: Now wait a minute. Do you make a habit of bursting into people's houses uninvited?

THIRD VISITOR (*a curly redhead, scantily skirted, with a habit of periodically patting her hair*) We knocked, dearie.

WIFE: Indeed? Wasn't that good of you, now. Well, Mr. Munbrane is busy.

REDHEAD: Call him Peter, dearie. We do.

WIFE (*starting in surprise*) Well, I *guess* I'll call him Peter, you — you —

BLACK HAIR: Don't say it, mops. (*She indicates the swarthy fellow with a jerk of her thumb.*) He told you we want to see Peter.

WIFE (*vehemently*) Well, you can't see him, so there. I — I don't think he's — very well —

SWARTHY: You're right, Ma'am, he isn't.

WIFE: He's been out of sorts for a week.

75

BLACK HAIR: Yeah, we know. (*WIFE looks startled.*)

WIFE: And the slightest disturbance irritates him. (*Her voice trembles.*) And he gets so worked up, and—and—(*She is on the verge of tears.*)

REDHEAD: There, there, dearie, we can fix things.

SWARTHY: We're going to fix things, all right.

BLACK HAIR: But good, the dumb—

WIFE: How dare you! I'll call the police. (*She glances quickly off stage to right.*)

BLACK HAIR, to REDHEAD: *She'll* call the police. Isn't that rich?

REDHEAD, to SWARTHY: Yeah, isn't that rich?

WIFE: Now, look. What is all this? What—

SWARTHY: He already called the police himself, see? We intercepted the call. He doesn't know what to do next. No wonder he's irritable.

BLACK HAIR: He thinks murder's cut and dried. The dumb—

WIFE: Oh, stop it! I won't have you—

BLACK HAIR (*to the other two, who have started to move towards the curtained-off corner*) She won't have us. Isn't that rich? (*WIFE follows them.*)

WIFE: Wait—you can't go in there.

As they approach the corner, a chair is heard to be pushed back sharply, and the curtain is whipped aside from within. A fellow with dishevelled hair, wearing an old sweatshirt and slacks, takes one step forward and stops dead. His mouth falls open. He stands transfixed.

THREE VISITORS (*each raising a hand*) Peter Munbrane. Hail!

WIFE: Peter, I couldn't help it. They burst in—

BLACK HAIR: Don't listen to her, Munbrane. We knocked. She knows we knocked. (*She turns to face WIFE.*)

SWARTHY and REDHEAD (*also turning*) Of course we knocked.

PETER MUNBRANE remains motionless, staring. The others turn and watch him closely. At last he moves slowly front, never taking his eyes off the visitors.

PETER (*in a shaken voice*) Just as I imagined them.

WIFE: Peter, who are these people? Do you know them?

REDHEAD: He should, dearie. Inside and out. (*WIFE looks at her sharply.*)

BLACK HAIR: If he'd left it to us—

REDHEAD: Yeah, who needs the police?

SWARTHY: Well, let's get at it. (*He leads the way as all three troop in behind the curtain. REDHEAD wiggles a hip and flicks the curtain closed.*)

WIFE: Oh, Peter, don't let them— (*She stops as a furious burst of typing begins. It continues for a full minute, uninterrupted except for the* ding *of the carriage bell and the* whack *of the carriage being returned.*)

PETER (*still shaken*) I—I can't believe it.

WIFE: Will you stop talking in riddles ? *What* can't you believe?

PETER: I might have known. I—might—have—known. (*He begins to laugh, getting louder and louder.*)

WIFE: Peter! Stop—stop—

PETER (*shouting*) It's going to work! It's going to work!

WIFE: Peter, you've *got* to listen to me.

PETER: I tried to push them around. I—

WIFE: Peter, you're sick. I'm going to end this nonsense right now. (*She hurries over to the curtain. The typing has already stopped, unnoticed in the uproar. She yanks the curtain open, then stands stock still.*)

WIFE: Peter!

PETER (*suddenly sobered*) What?

WIFE: There's—nobody there. (*PETER tiptoes over and joins her. The corner is quite deserted. Of course, the three occupants could have slipped through a hidden exit built into the set. Or, could they?*)

PETER: Did you see them go?

WIFE: How could I see anything at all, with you carrying on like a maniac? Did *you* see them go?

PETER: I sure did not. But—look. (*He goes in. There is a sound of paper being yanked out of a typewriter. In a few moments he reappears, reading it. His face breaks into a broad grin, then he starts laughing again.*)

WIFE: Peter, be sane. I can't stand it—

PETER (*between uproarious bursts of laughter*) It's all fixed. Fixed, I tell you. It's just what I needed. Oh joy—oh, glory. I should have done it all along.

WIFE: Done what, you fool? Done what?

PETER: (*by now almost hysterical*) What they all tell you to do. 'Let your characters write your story.' It's the only rule there is!

WIFE: That old saw! Say, are you trying to suggest—?

PETER: It works, it works! (*Now quite out of control, he does a whirling dance, then collapses into a chair and falls forward with his face on the table. WIFE comes slowly towards the front of the non-stage, spreading both hands as though in resignation.*)

WIFE (*to non-audience*) You see what I have to live with?

(Quick non-curtain)

DAT